FATHER

Other books by Jeff Daniel Marion —

Out in the Country, Back Home, Jackpine Press, 1976
Tight Lines, Iron Mountain Press, 1981
Vigils, Appalachian Consortium Press, 1990
Lost & Found, Sow's Ear Press, 1994
The Chinese Poet Awakens, Wind Publications, 1999
Letters Home, Sow's Ear Press, 2001
Ebbing & Flowing Springs, Celtic Cat Publishing, 2002

Hello, Crow, Orchard Books, 1992 (children's book)

FATHER

Jeff Daniel Marion

Jeff Daniel Marion

WIND PUBLICATIONS

International Standard Book Number 978-1-893239-90-6
Library of Congress Control Number 2009920560

First edition

Front cover photo: "Waiting" © Jeff Daniel Marion

Acknowledgments

This volume includes poems from other volumes as noted:

Out in the Country, Back Home, Jackpine Press, © 1976
Vigils, Appalachian Consortium Press, © 1990
Lost & Found, Sow's Ear Press, © 1994
Letters Home, Sow's Ear Press, © 2001
Ebbing & Flowing Springs, Celtic Cat Publishing, © 2002

The author offers grateful acknowledgement to the editors of these presses and to the editors of the following periodicals in which some of these poems originally appeared: *Appalachian Heritage, Appalachian Journal, Atlanta Review, Blink, Blue Fifth Review, The Distillery, Grist, Pembroke Magazine, Pisgah Review, Poet Lore, Puddingstone, Roanoke Review, The Southern Review*, and *Tar River Poetry.*

For sound advice and loving encouragement in the writing of these poems, I wish to thank my wife Linda and my son Stephen. I also wish to thank my long-time friend Ted Kooser, who first suggested the idea for this book in 1993. Special thanks go to Doug Berryhill for his invaluable help in the electronic preparation of the manuscript for this volume. Finally, my gratitude goes to Charlie Hughes, editor at Wind Publications, for his belief that this work was worthy of publication.

For the memory of my father

J. D. Marion

1915-1990

Contents

III

IV

FARM SCENE, 1918

The three-year-old boy squinches his eyes, left hand
tucked inside overalls too short for him; barefoot
on the running board, he stands between his father's legs,
the father overalled too, his right hand lifted, holding
to the canopy post of the Model T Ford truck,
where he sits looking out from the passenger's seat.
The boy's cousin, older, leans against the truck,
his bandana just lifted from his hip pocket.
Young as they are, they are already weathered as the pine
bark slabs stacked on the truck bed, late September
ripe with resin scent, wooden spoke wheels and hard
rubber tires ready to roll to market, the crank
hanging loose at the front, its lightning
kickback strong as the engine's throb: now piston
thrust into a future past these crackling
parched cornfields, hauling harvest down hard-
baked clay roads of East Tennessee toward a day
of blue snow seventy-two years later but quick
as the engine's spark when the once-overalled-boy's hands
tuck across his chest lapped in satin and he is lowered
into the frozen ground where his own son now
stands above him, his breath throbbing:
O Father.

1

I

LULLABY, 1943

They roll up the rug to waltz
to Wayne King, the record
spilling its black platter
of music across the living
room, shuffle and slide of shoes
as the couples sway together:
my mother and father, Nick
and Issie, Chick and Dorothy,
voices adrift on the late
night hour and I in my child's
bed, listening, turn back and
forth. Nearby on my parents'
bed, coats and scarves lie still,
waiting, facing the window
where, outside, snow swirls its slow
dance and the world spins through dark.

LUNCHBOX

Black rounded top like a train,
an old steam engine waiting
at station, kitchen table
sidestop: my mother loads it
for the daily run, Detroit
City from the Projects on
Midgarden line traveling
to Alcoa plant where my
father works, will unload his
cargo at whistle's noon call:
wedge of cornbread, thermos full
of coffee, bowl of soup beans,
sometimes a sausage biscuit.

"What kind of food is this?" friends
want to know, Poles and Czechs who
work by his side. "Home," he says.
"Some good old mountain cooking."

In the long afternoons my
mother puts me to bed, nap
time: "Let's get on a train, go
home to see Grandma Lucy
and Dollie in Tennessee."
"We don't have tickets, honey.
Now close your eyes, go to sleep."

Dreams rock me, rock me,
down lines of leafy trees, rolling hills,
apple blossoms floating till

I wake rubbing sleep from my
eyes, wander into kitchen
where the lunchbox has come back.

I unsnap the latches, lift
the lid to see what's aboard –
little toy or treat, Daddy
brought home for me as he does
each day on this treasure train.

A SATURDAY NIGHT, 1944

My father fiddles the knobs
of our Philco, screech to
squawk as the green dial rakes
across stations, the static
of distance hissing before
he fine-tunes the music from
Nashville, the Grand Ole Opry.
To the twang of banjo he
strikes a match with his thumbnail,
cups his hands around the flame,
lights his Lucky. He pats
his foot as voices flock
round the cigarette's red glow,
his little lantern swung back
and forth through this faraway
dark, signal calling over
mountains to the blue valleys,
curling smoke from the homefires,
wings of song settled down there.

BELLE ISLE PARK, 1944

War rages on, my father's three
brothers far away at sea,
but this Sunday, in early May
my mother, my father, and I
stare into the future's eye, fixed
before a fountain within a fountain,
the three of us posed on the rim
of a basin like the ledge of the present
soon to fall forever past.
My father frowns, his two-toned
wingtips newly buffed, polished,
shirt cuffs turned up two folds, tie
askew to left, felt hat cocked
at jaunty angle. Between them,
I lean toward my mother, her left arm
behind me, right in lap, caressing my arm.
Her striped spring dress and dark hair
billow slightly in wind.
I am happy in this outing,
loving the marble lion
towering behind us, live
turtle scrambling from water
to safe perch, loving all things
behind and before us in
this moment when the shutter
clicks, my aunt has said *Smile* and
I'm the only one who does.

TICKET STUB, 1944

He kept it all these years, stub
from a ticket tucked in
a box shelved in his junkhouse.
Now it springs green in my hand:
Monday, May 29, 1944, moment
when my father, home from work,
smiles to say he is going
to see the Tigers play, his
one chance to watch major league,
far cry from cow pasture games
back in the mountains, left field
bounded by scraggly patch of
woods, feedsack bases, flat rock home
plate. Soon to be four, I look
up to him, stripes of color
already dancing, orange,
black and white, grace of cats, sleek
and leaping, rolling in what
surely would be greenest grass,
living proof of what I had
seen in my children's book, purr
of pages turning with stroke
of my mother's hand. "Take me,
take me," I pleaded, only
to hear, "Just one ticket, buddy.
Some other time." I cried and
cried until Mama put me
to bed, the long afternoon
a fitful tossing, turning,
tigers out of reach, safe in

their stadium, my father
cheering them on, waving his
hat in this palace of wonder,
world of war momentarily
forgotten. Back home early
evening, hint of summer
surrounding his circle, friends
gathered on the lawn, red glow
of cigarettes dot the dark,
Cy and Lois, Nick, Issie,
Fred and Pearl. Snug between my
father's legs, I am given
a swig from his beer, tingle
of his drink on my lips. He
tips his bottle in salute:
"To brothers at sea, the end
of this war, Memorial Day, and
to the Tigers, three cheers
for all!" I lean back in his
arms, voices lifting in cheer,
visions of my father and
me gazing out upon fields
stretching far beyond this dark,
into kingdoms where tigers play.

VICTORY GARDEN, 1945

My mother bends in the row,
lifts hoe to chop another
weed, remembers when her man
ahead, bent to bucket's heft,
was the boy who swore no more
sweat off his brow to plow
down rows, no more nettles to sting
like bees needling barefoot arch,
no more breaking his back for
a measly mess of greens, beans
by the bushel to break, string
until fingers go numb, no.
Just look at us now, loving
what once we hated, far off
from mountains on this flat
patch of dirt they let us tend,
my mother muses. Father picks
greens, basket brimful, his feast
already a taste he can
savor, pot liquor stewed long,
seasoned right, smelling of home.
My father bends in the row,
beans blooming, promise of more.

THE CALL, 1945

War behind us, my father
sleeps late on a Saturday,
dreams of a morning in May
back in the mountains, chores done.
Wind sighs in the long, leafy
arms of willow. Faraway
clink of trace chains, his father
hitching horses, my father
waking to call of three knocks
from our apartment door, rouses
to hop across cold floor, hear:
"You J. D. Marion?"
stranger's stare demands, offers
"You got a long distance call
down at the phone." My mother
watches him bound down the steps
and cross the street to the only
telephone in our section
of the Projects. Sure trouble
back home, maybe message of
death brought by this stranger, why
else this call? My mother hugs
her bathrobe closer, shivers
to see him cradle the cold
receiver, listen to voice
crackle across six hundred
miles. Back upstairs my father
grins. "Wake that boy and roust him
out – sweet mountains here we come.
They called to offer my old

job back!" His grin fades, a new
cloud of mystery, before
saying, "I forgot to thank
him." He shakes his head, tongue
clucking. "There'll be plenty
of time when we're home," she says.
"No, no, not *him* – that stranger
we'll never see again
who took the call and gave us
our ticket to Tennessee."

CHRISTMAS FIREWORKS, 1948

All day they soaked the softballs,
rag wrapped, tightly bound wads,
in kerosene so that come evening
and the fall of blue dark, they
stood in the streets, our fathers
in mackinaws and leather work gloves,
their shouted words patches of smoke
lifting across the icy distances of neighborhood.

All this to hurl great flames across the sky
to one another, to get their fill of catching
shooting stars, to laugh at the darkness
shot through with arcing fiery fastballs,
our blazing ornaments of memory.

MY FATHER LIGHTS ANOTHER LUCKY

Leaning back in his easy
chair, head resting on doily,
my father lights another
Lucky, takes a long drag, then
exhales, its blue plume rising
through halo of lamplight, long
day uncurling in moment's
satisfaction. I climb
to his lap, laugh at smoke
I cannot grasp. He puffs rings
round my arm – one, two, three –
bracelets slipping away.
        So many
years ago he quit smoking,
my mother tells, because I
kept reaching for his glowing
cigarette. What I wished for
lived in the magic cup of
his hands, a hut where some genie
chugged smoke through the chimney
of his thumbs, doors of fingers
opened and *poof* he disappeared,
a trick I fell for time and
time again until now when
there is no sleight of hand, no
smoke to cloud the truth of his
vanishing, death's lucky strike.

THE BOX

Sportee Sox: rectangular
box, faded green with yellow
sailboats drifting, two-story
mansion on the distant shore.
Here the bits and pieces of
my father's early working
days reside: mileage ration
card for a 1936 Chevrolet
coupe issued to J. D. Marion,
3001 1/2 Lycaste, Detroit, Mich.,
11-19-42, basement two-room
apartment unheated, soon
condemned, sending us to live
in Herman Gardens Projects
where one morning he found his
coupe propped on Coke crates, wheels gone;
Draft Classification 2B,
three brothers shipped to far ends
of South Pacific, only
he and sister left behind;
United Steel Workers dues
card, stamps still neatly glued in
place; brass badge #I769,
Aluminum Castings Co.,
reminder of days molding
pistons for PT boats, sweat
for the war effort so strong
on one of his buddies, they
shoved him into shower stall,

scrubbed him down with bristle brush;
Alcoa cigarette ration
card, pack of Luckies his choice,
each slender wand tapped on the face
of his wristwatch; folded top half
of statement form, address from
Walter Kazol, his old friend,
who year after year long past
our Detroit days sent Christmas
greetings, present of book or
puzzle for me. Now I sort
through these jigsaw pieces, try
to place each within some frame:
Projects where we lived torn
down, streets renamed, no photos
to prompt those few memories,
how do I construct, save some
picture from this past fading
to dust? The day of his dying
I swore to remember, his
body sinking beneath white
sheets and later cold blue snow
swirling as his box sank past
sight. Today I hold tatters
for a few moments, lift them
back to their box, yellowed sheets
of time sailing on, bound for
far shores only words can reach.

II

RINGER

Come July dusk amid rasp
and whine of jarflies' song,
day's work done, they gathered, fathers
of the neighborhood, to pitch
horseshoes, have a smoke, laugh till
night drove them in. Already
lights coming on in row
of white clapboard houses, clink
of supper dishes done, calls
from screened backdoors to come home,
we lingered just one more round
to be near the men, listen
to the game's talk. Even now
their voices ring across dark
deeper than dream: Virgil, Pete,
Junior, Zack, my own father
J. D., names that clang like a
horseshoe on steel, each boy in
that timeless summer hoping
to be pegged the lucky one
by hearing: "Boy, damned if you
and your dad ain't dead ringers."

OIL CANS

Like birds perched in a line,
they sat side by side, smallest
to largest, their long copper beaks
poised and ready. Whatever
squeak or rattle called, my father's
hand darted, hovered and dipped
to deliver healing balm,
left hinge or wheel free to fly
smooth as the whisper of wings.

PENNED

Hour by hour the howls, baying
beagles my father brought home,
housed in a wire-fenced run, ten-
by-six strip soon made smooth by
this pacing pair hungry for
scent of zig-zag runners,
blue roil of gunsmoke on November's
crisp air. First, they dug their way
out, pawing mounds to tunnel,
fat little groundhogs loping
through yards, ears laid back, flopping
in the wind. Then Pat, smaller
of the two, learned to nose
the gate latch up and open, fresh
trails again over the mowed
grass of neighborhood. This time
my father swore to keep them
in, spring so strong on the latch,
Pat's nose rubbed raw before he
learned fence climbing, ladder rungs
of wire lifting him, solo
flight to leave Mike behind,
squawl of prisoner too much to
bear even for my father,
that strict formalist who sent
them to a cousin's farm, let
loose to ramble the crisscross
of cowtrails, chase every
scent for twelve weeks before they
came back, tongues lolling, their

arched ribcage a lean pen for
hunger's edge, panting in the cool
space under the front porch floor,
hunters seasoned and ready,
taste whetted by running free,
my father grinning, chastened.

STOP ME IF . . .

My father, sly grinner, would say,
"Times were so hard back then
I could step on a dime and tell
whether it was heads or tails,"
his unshod feet quick to read
whatever terrain he trod.

"Poor as Job's turkey we had
to take down one of our windmills –
couldn't afford wind for both.
But we had our own kind of fun –
a talking mule who flicked his tail
at hard times, his one word
when asked how many shucks
he wanted: *Few*."

THE ORDAINING

My father knelt at the front
of the sanctuary, eyes closed,
waiting. One by one deacons
filed past: E. S. Clifton, the town's
jeweler, white brush mustache,
hands pale and palsied, trembled
a moment before they swept
over my father's head like fingers
appraising a fine sculpture;
Bill Davis of Citizens Supply, keeper
of a lumberyard stacked with pallets
of fir, white and yellow pine, whose hands
measured in spans and cubic feet,
always ready to reach for the carpenter's
pencil lodged behind his right ear,
now marked the smooth contour
of my father's bald head; Ray Price
who could fine-tune any engine
to a silky purr, knuckles dark with ground-
in grease, stain that shone beyond
his dress shirt's starched cuffs;
Brady Gladson, hardware store clerk,
who knew the heft and balance of the best
claw hammer, double-bitted axe, scoops
and bins of ten-penny nails, catalog
of what held the world together, what
would mend the broken, couple the separate
pieces, hands flitting like wings of a butterfly;
and Dennie Payne, county court clerk,

whose delicate script with a fountain pen
swirled and stood upright, letter by letter
filling the leather-bound ledgers, cupped
his hands firmly on my father's bowed
head. Touch by touch they anointed him
with the oil of their palms, the living cup
of their hands offering the grit and grace
of their days, work of the flesh made holy
to lift him up to stand one among the chosen.

THE MAN WHO LOVED HUMMINGBIRDS

Once I saw my father
        lift from last fall's leaves
                below our wide picture window

a hummingbird, victim
        of reflected surfaces, the one clue
                a single feather clinging above the sill.

He cradled its body in his cupped
        hands and breathed across the fine
                iridescent chest and ruby throat.

I remembered all the times
        his hands became birdcalls, whistles,
                crow's caw from a blade of grass.

Then the bird stirred and rose
        to perch on his thumb.
                As he slowly raised his hand

the wings began to hum
        and my father's breath lifted
                and flew out across the world.

MY FATHER'S WATCH, 1950

An Omega, among the best, sure
to keep time running right
on the money, Mr. Clifton said,
scrawling a receipt in the slow
but steady hand of a third-
generation jeweler, trade passed
from grandfather to father to son
now in his seventies. The watch
gleamed on the counter, leather
band and round face a perfect
circle waiting. My father studied
the Greek letter in gold, a little
good luck horseshoe arched
over twelve, starting point for
lickety-split gallop of seconds into
minutes, race to the finish line
to begin again, first to last.
An Omega bought on time,
Mr. Clifton winked, and my father
strapped it on, heart pounding,
step quickened to this pace of time,
his first new watch and last.

THE BOYS AT THE INK ROOM,
INTERNATIONAL PLAYING CARD & LABEL CO.

You always called them that, no matter
everyone was well past thirty, time held
in abeyance for the memory of youth
long gone, those days on the farm
before coming to town for some job
other than following a mule's ass sunup
to sundown, swatting flies and sweat bees,
the swiping cuts from blades of corn,
the burning sting of an occasional packsaddle.

Now the boys – Esau Epps and Jim Chapman,
Curly Bloomer and Curt Lipe – come to work
amid towers of leaning buckets labeled
with names they know by heart: Van Camp red,
Chesterfield green and Bugler blue, Lucky Strike
silver and Phillip Morris gold. The smell
of solvents blends with the whir of blades
when colors swirl and mix in vats,
batches of rainbows the boys carry home
on shirt and pants, their wives knowing
it's the permanent palette of work, the stain
no amount of washing would ever make clean,
color the lasting clock to mark their time.

In honor of the Clifton clock on Main Street
by which the town told time, one of the boys
painted a white bucket lid with hands forever
fixed at 3 p.m. and C-I-L-F-T-O-N

as CLIFTON misspelled, quitting time for all
to see. When complaints came about the slowness
of a worker, the accused always pointed
to the lid-clock and claimed he was on overtime,
double pay due for such devoted and hard work,
service above and beyond the call of duty
for the boys at the ink room.

MY FATHER'S TACKLEBOX

The shiny metal latches
snap crisp as the lid springs back:
here are all the little rooms
where his fishing trips rest, tales
of topwater casting with
jitterbug, its frog body
chugging the surface to froth,
wavelets sent out to signal
bass to swirl beneath and strike,
burst into the world's bubble
of air and dance, scales a shimmer
of silver, divining rod
arched and pulsing in his hand
which on another day might
choose skipjack, its rolling
B-B rattle sure to lure
a lazy largemouth to bite –
all the ways to witch a spell
wait here: rooster tail feather
fluff hiding treble barbed hooks,
hand-tied Popeye flies, broken-
back Rappala minnows, lead
sinkers and plastic bobbers
for the dog days of summer
when only bluegill will be
beguiled, all others safe, tucked
in their deep pockets of home.

MY FATHER BELIEVED IN BIRDS

My father believed in birds,
especially the return
of purple martins, flocked

to high-rise apartments he
mounted on poles, dutifully
took down each winter to clean,

waiting for spring when he raised
them again, beacons calling
his welcome across the miles:

*Come iridescent flash, swerve
and dive, find home here above
garden's loop, tendril, and vine.*

So went their ritual year
after year until that time
he forgot, lost in the days'

hard demands, and they gathered,
these migrants lining telephone
wires, rooftops, circling where houses

once were, generations drawn
back to perch and nest now gone.
In the labor of that day's dusk

I see him still, amid cries
and wings' flurry, his hands
lifting high a welcome home.

MOURNING DOVE

My father, the crack shot,
laid down his sixteen-gauge
at the sound of the lost mate
calling and cooing across the crisp
October afternoon, the cornfield's
pale parchment growing silent.
He spoke of it only once,
but I have wondered these many
years what he heard in that
plaintive note – whether whistle
cry of a train passing in the night,
emptiness surrounding that simple sound,
or perhaps something deeper yet
like the unspeakable recoil of grief.

INK BUCKETS

Stacked head-high and leaning left
they looked like three towers of Pisa
there in the back of his junkhouse,
white plastic cast-offs he stowed away
from work, these buckets nestled
among tarps and two-by-fours,
enough to supply neighbors'
needs, friends, farmers whose calls
my mother tallied on a notepad:
Clay Price – Choptack – ten buckets,
Renn Lawson – Guntown – five buckets,
Elsie Goins – St. Clair – two buckets,
and so the roll call went,
my father's bucket brigade,
I called them, out at sunrise
slopping the hogs, toting water
for the horses, slinging mash
for the chickens, pouring sweetfeed
into the trough, their arms bulging
from the heft and hoist of bucket
after bucket, their hands stained
by earth's dark ink.
"A man can never have enough,"
my father said, gravelling
potatoes from the garden, piling
high the mound, listing to the weight
of harvest he hauled down the rows,
his buckets filled to the brim.

WASTE NOT

Believing Ecclesiastes spoke true,
my father toted them home, knowing
to every thing there is a season, tail
ends of paper rolls tossed from
printing presses where he worked,
saved from the scrap heap, these
wide sheets rich with the hues
of Old Gold, Pall Mall red, Lucky
Strike green, Sir Walter Raleigh brown,
silver from some unknown source.
Lined in rows in the back of his
junkhouse, they stood erect waiting
the proper occasion: white to line
kitchen shelves, home to pink
Depression glass; Bugler's blue
for the dresser drawers, cool little
lakes for our clothes to float on;
come Fourth of July the paper
unfurled like a cloth on the picnic
table for the glory of a rattlesnake melon,
crackling open its red heart, those spewed
seeds like black stars on deep blue;
week after week summer's bounty
offered, a still life of Big Boy tomatoes
on a canvas of silver, yellow crook-
neck squash against green, Aunt Verdie's
banana pudding in a pale lemon bowl

on gold. But best of all against
winter's drab gray below our
Christmas tree a rainbow of wrappings,
my father the wise man grinning,
spreading his wealth, wasting not.

J. D. M.

Remembering their names
my father recounts the days,
each one mapped deep
in his memory. He believes
I remember them all,
have known them in my own way.

Listening, I settle back
and find the places in his voice:
an old cemetery, its gate rusty,
the air heavy with the incense of cedars.
He names those friends once more
and I choose the grave stone
for each, study the lines growing faint.

Savoring the tales he tells,
he resurrects them one by one.
They do a strange dance
shaped by his words
and for a moment I believe
I knew them, shared their days.

We turn off the main road,
wind back in the mountains
toward Galbraith Springs.
People came from far places
believing this water a cure.
As a boy he and his friends came here
to sell blackberries and listen

to stories of other places,
a map of the world growing wider
summer by summer.

No one comes here much anymore.

But this is his place:
quiet and forgotten,
his youth lies buried here,
marked only by his initials
carved into a wooden bench
set beside the spring.

We eye one another across shadows
darkening the spring. We search for
some word that could cure,
heal us now in this moment passing.
The only sound is the spring, quietly flowing.

He kneels, cups his hands to drink
and believes what he has always told me:
"Some springs never go dry."

III

A SHORT HISTORY OF MUSIC

My father remembers the rhythm
    of steel on steel, the spikes
        driven by black men

laying the rails to the chanted
    tune of an old song.
        These days when the mourning

dove calls, he swears he hears
    the echo of trains passing,
        the lament of their lonesome whistle.

What I remember is waiting at night
    twenty years ago near the crossing
        with my son listening to the boxcar beat

of clacketa-clack, clack-clack.
    Now coming home I hear the clatter
        of his typewriter keys and swear

I've traveled this line before
    down tracks with only a whistle
        to my name.

78 RPM

In the back of the junkhouse
stacked on a cardtable covered
by a ragged bedspread, they rest,
black platters whose music once
crackled, hissed with a static
like shuffling feet, fox trot or two-step,
the slow dance of the needle
riding its merry-go-round,
my mother's head nestled
on my father's shoulder as they
turned, lost in the sway of sounds,
summer nights and faraway
places, the syncopation of time
waltzing them to a world
they never dreamed, dance
of then to the dust of now.

AND SO THE TIME GOES

My father asks if I have time
       to wind the clock, his days
              bound by tubes looping

across his face to bring the next
       breath. I listen to his slow rasp,
              the bubbles perking from his oxygen.

I take the key and turn clockwise,
       then counterclockwise as
              the ratchet of time rewinds.

In this turning memory retrieves
       a day forty years ago
              when we rafted into a summer noon.

We rode the rising currents free
       as birds soaring past the next bend,
              slipping out of sight.

Now what I am learning is to live
       wholly in the moment, to fear
              not death, but dying, the unwinding

that empties our bodies of joy.
       I have wound the clock,
              good father, your hands palsied

with patchy bruises blue
       as storm clouds beneath the skin.
              The steady pendulum swings on,

and I know the hard truth is
      only when death is ready
           will your wings unfold

to lift you free
      beyond this dark weather,
           beyond time.

INK ROOM

Rows of buckets stacked head-high,
their labels a litany
of color: Pall Mall red, Van
Camp tan, Chesterfield green and
Bluebird blue, swatches of hues
spread with a drawdown knife beside
their names, each a formula
my father filed in memory.
They hustle around the rows,
Curt the right-hand man quick to
learn his secrets and Esau,
rubber gauntlet gloves up to
his elbows, sloshing buckets
in their bath of lye, scrubbing
dried patches of rainbow-swirl
away to bring back the shine,
eager to be home, hands
deep in his garden's black ink.
They knew my father by trade,
the master of shades, subtle
blends mixed in huge vats, his shirt
and pants a palette of day's
work, the smell of kerosene
and solvents my mother swore
never would come clean, never
would wash out, the place marking
him, its stain indelible
in the clothes my mother folds
to give away, her fingers
lingering over all that's
left of him to remember.

MY FATHER'S SHOES

"Much obliged," I can still hear
him say, a Saturday afternoon in town,
the old ways unfolding, formal
but kindly. Meeting a friend – man or woman –
he always tipped his hat,
the whisper of his wingtips
lifting him away, his step
jaunty and sure.

I never asked what memories
lay hidden in his closet whose floor
was a parade ground ready for inspection:
row after row of mostly Florsheims –
oxblood, midnight green, brown and black,
wing on wing on wing with occasional loafers,
dress boots, house slippers, comfortable old friends.

"Be glad you've got good shoes
and keep them shined," I heard,
staring down at my Buster Browns.
Every Saturday night he buffed
and polished, the shine-rag popping
until his face gleamed back at him.

Twenty years later I got the picture,
him barefoot and lucky to have one
pair of shoes a year, to be worn only
in winter, strips of groundhog hide
fashioned for laces.

How many times did I hear
the one about the boy whose soles
were so thin he could step on a dime
and tell whether it was heads or tails?

"What did he want with all these shoes?"
My mother wrings her hands
and worries, "What will we do with them?"

I want to say, "There's no one – not now,
not ever – to fill them," but instead
I'm dreaming of a place where heaven
is a string of Saturday afternoons,
my father's '47 Chevrolet sleek and gleaming
at the curb beside Home Service.
All his friends have crossed over
to linger in the shade of City Drug,
its canvas awning blue and tan.
They lift their hands as he calls:
O Buck, Tommy Bruce, Roger.
O the wars are all over
and we have come home at last
to shoot the breeze, to tell the old jokes
over again, to laugh and wile away the time,
to loaf on these familiar streets forever.

A VISIT TO MY FATHER'S GRAVE
IN FEBRUARY

This we do in remembrance:
my mother and I walk
past row after row of identical markers
until we come to the end,
a single bronze plaque on the ground.

I study the hills beyond
where maple and dogwood cling
to the ridges, their buds
tight fists against the cold.

No stones, no marble angels,
no reclining lambs,
only two crows.
Old black-robed scholars,
you will read no wisdom
here, only a list of names
sweeping silently from one end
to the other of this grave yard.

Removing the red plastic roses,
I lift the vase from its cup,
pour out the rainwater.
Slivers of ice cling to the stems.
No canker, no rust, no mold.

"I've never seen a place so cold."
My mother arranges the artificial

dogwood branches, their blush-tipped petals
quivering in the wind.

We turn back to the waiting car,
leaving behind these little flags
of remembrance where we have staked
our claim, a name on the ground,
and a bouquet of blooms
that will not die.

THE MAN WHO MADE COLOR

Consider the lilies, we have been told,
they toil not,
neither do they labor.

But I have sweated in the fall sun
to plant this hillside
in a cascade of hues, held
in a ring of rocks I have carried
from the river.

Long ago on my first day of school,
the teacher asked, "What does your father do?"
"He makes color," I said.
"Oh ... I see."

But she did not see the man
who stood before vats of color
deep as flame
and dipped his finger in,
touching paper, testing the tack
of ink.

I saw him believe in the truth
of touch, the message only his fingers
would tell, color splashing
across rolling sheets of labels:
Bugler, Del Monte, Van Camp,
School Days, Lucky Strike.

Consider these lilies, Father, their color
a swash of words I roll across
my tongue – *Harbor Blue, Open Hearth,*
Spindazzle, Kindly Light. They sway
on their long stems but a day.
They know no grief, no loss,
only a tumble of color,
season to season, across this hillside.
Their blossoms unfold bright as flame,
ready for your touch.

STILL WATERS

There we are, fishing on a farm pond
in June, two men in a small boat
christened *Satisfied Mind*, an old sheepdog
sprawled asleep between us,
sky the neon blue of a dragonfly.

Here we are safe, father and son
taking turns with the paddle, slipping
with the ease of a water strider.

What matters now is the plop
of a plastic worm, its wiggle
to the depths and the ripples
lapping back.

Time seems to hold its breath, waiting
the moment's nibble, nothing more
than a cork float to watch
as it bobs, sinks, rises again.

Rocked in the boat of satisfaction, we drift.

The bluebirds break our revery,
skimming the sky's reflection, their frantic dive
and swerve to save the nestlings
who have fallen from first flight to this watery world.

Listening to their repeated cries, I forgive you
all my childhood hurts.

You lift a drowned nestling on the paddle,
then let it drift down to its grave.

On that day, years before your cancer,
before my divorce, son to father,
father to father, how could I know then
these still waters cannot save us?

Even now as I stand by your grave,
I search for words to rescue, cast lines
to waters whose currents I can only guess,
rowing toward the future.

MY FATHER'S UNICORN

My father's unicorn was a spotted
mule, rare enough to make *Ripley's*
Believe It or Not, smack in the middle
of the funny papers. He was the jack-
pot, end-of-the-line, million-to-one
chancy roll of genetic dice –

this marker my father always noted traveling
Lee Highway just outside Blaine, Tennessee:
better than any beast the zoo could offer,
this gee-haw miracle of a farmboy's dreams.

Now some fifty years later I pass
that spot, stare beyond the empty
field's horizon. Clouds roll back
like furrows and still my father's
words plow on: *Look quick, son,*
and I do, both forward and back,
harnessed to memory.

STRIPE RUN, MARCH 1977

Where Cloud's Creek joins the Holston,
my father yells "Hadacol"
to his brother ten yards down
river: "My line's busy – call
later." These two wrestle zig
and zag of bass, current pull,
lean to and back, heave and reel
to bring to light the silver
flash, gills' red sawtooth rasping,
slap and flop of striped body
on silty bank. Home they hoist
metal stringers glistening
for the camera's one eye.
This is how I see them now:
grinning, squinting into late
afternoon's glare, their lives caught
in a moment's victory –
years before cancer snagged both,
reeled them in stilled beneath heave
of red clay, stone's weathered lines.

AIRBORNE

I

How would it be, we wondered,
boys reliving the war stories
brought home by uncles, fathers,
neighbors, to see at 12 o'clock high,
a Zero on your tail and time
now with black smoke billowing
to bail out, trust that ripcord,
faith in a silky bloom to float
you down into enemy territory?
And so we jumped, tiny cargo
parachute in hand, from the twelve-
foot drop of Chester Smith's front porch,
feet stinging like a thousand needles,
tumbling in clouds of dust, sky
ablaze with July, P-40 Flying Tiger
lost in the mirage of time.

II

My father's idea – "I'm taking the boy up,"
he winked at my frowning mother,
"Duke Mayes will fly us over the neighborhood –
maybe he'll buzz the house and tip his wing
so you'll know it's us." We all knew
of Daredevil Duke and his Piper Cub:
the day he soared under Austin Mill
bridge, strafing the fishing boats,
Popeye Leonard swearing that damned old Duke
had given him a flattop and the first

clean shave he'd had all week, then
scaled and filleted a three-pound
largemouth as his prop skimmed
the surface of the Holston.

Duke gave one backward flip
of the propeller and the engine fired,
fescue bowing in the Choptack pasture.
We bumped over clods,
earth giving way toward the welcoming
horizon, hills and knobs
unfurling like a green flag before
the world went sigoglin in a steep
bank left and we looked down on
the dots of neighborhood,
felt the hard tug of gravity,
the claim of ground begging us back.

III

Sixty Octobers now and still
I startle at the sight: the blaze
and ruin of fall, milkweed pods empty,
abandoned fuselages of the field,
their silky seeds given up to float
like parachutes on the wind
past the graves of them all:
father, uncles, neighbors grounded here,
their stories airborne on
a single breath into the blue distance.

IV

HOWITZER SHELL

My father rescued it from
the crawlspace beneath our first
house, brass relic some soldier
toted home, left to canker.
Saved to be base for a lamp
my father dreamed, come summer
I lugged it out of the junkhouse
across the yard and up the mimosa
limbs, ready to fly my mission,
crouched among the flaming red
blooms of anti-aircraft fire,
my target in the yard below –
Hail to Hitler – bombs away!
and the B-29 soared back
to home base on the sweet scent
of July. War games over,
the shell waited to be lamp,
upright in the corner,
until the day Buddy died.
Tan fur his everyday uniform –
soldier, traveler, hobo among hobos –
we rolled him to the garden
in a red wheelbarrow, tolled
his passing with twelve strokes
of a hammer on the shell,
its knell darkening the day.

THE GIFT

December, 1962, and you came to visit,
downtown Gay Street swept by snowy
winds as we walked toward my favorite
shop of used books on the corner of Summit.
No exchange of names, but the storekeeper
knew me well, had seen me savor
the smell and texture of ancient pages,
history of previous owners' musings
scribbled in margins, bold names scrawled
across colored endpapers. That day he offered
a bargain, *A Report on the Recent Revolution
in the Colonies,* Dublin, 1782. I thumbed
the brittle and foxed sheets, lingered
over the ligatures joining *s* and *t*,
the *f*s like a smooth swirl of *S*.
You stared at the storekeeper,
"How much?" and I studied you
weighing the ten dollars "today's price"
like a full bag of groceries, two weeks
worth of gasoline, or better yet a shiny
new pair of Florsheim wingtips.
I passed the book to you, plunged
my hands in empty pockets.
"Would you like to have it?"
I heard you whisper and read
those raised brows, lines of your face
always puzzled by my years of using
half a week's allotment for food
to buy books. You lifted a crisp
new bill to pay, cradled the book in my hands

like an offering laid on the altar of misspent
youth. Only days before Christmas I pocketed
this early present, mumbled thanks.
What strings bound this gift –
the glittering eye of a shrewd salesman?
Years of unease between father and son?
A wish to make amends?
Something darker from your past?
After New Year's I returned
to the shop, the owner index-finger-pecking
on a battered Royal typewriter, his passion
to write novels the likes of Zane Grey,
Riders of the Purple Sage the model he quoted,
eyes distant and searching some faraway
dream. The keys went silent for a moment
and I heard him say what I never told,
"December was a hard month – say thanks
to your father from my wife and me.
That ten dollars put Christmas dinner on the table."

TO MY FATHER TEN YEARS LATER

I

How weak my words seemed then, frail
birds come to perch on bare limbs,
feathers fluffed, hunched and huddled
beneath a sky spitting blue snow on
the day of your dying, O longest night.

II

Six months later you visited:
a hospital bed in a windowless
room, you lay beneath the white
sheet of final winter, a stillness
I could not fathom. You rose, slinging
the sheet back and I ran to
your side, both hands pushing you down,
back onto the bed where
you belonged: *I've got to
get out of here*, harsh words
ringing as I woke and stumbled
from my bed into the summer
night, cold and distant light of stars
still burning, river still whispering.

III

That same year you visited again:
we drove in the old '47 Chevrolet,
you and I in front,
Uncle Gene in back, and

arrived at the vacant lot,
neighborhood gathering place
for tag football, Sunday softball.
It was late fall, almost November, grass
still green, a cool crisp afternoon,
but I was snug in my dreams
of fourteen, wondering where my friends
were, waiting for the game to begin.
I heard your voice and turned
to see that you and Gene were
outside: *Let the bear out*, you had said.
I felt its black bulk push past me,
slime of drool on my arm, heavy
earthiness of bear's odor filling the car.
Gene leaned on the rear fender whittling
a cedar stick and you watched
the shavings curl and fall, the bear
wallowing nearby in the grass.
Left in the car, I did not belong
in that field beyond time where
you had wandered, your world safe
from me, the drowsy sprawl of
afternoon, the long sleep coming on.

      IV

I don't hear from you much anymore,
the three of you leaving no forwarding
address. I am left here with my words,
those black birds gathering on this field
of white, wings ready for the long flight,
homing signals stirring darkly within.

PRAYER TO A DEAD FATHER

Father, I never forgave you
those lessons to learn my ABC's
at three, trembling and peeing
my pants in fear of not
pleasing you, your scowl a red
welt stinging. Not till fourth grade
could I say them through, lined
like wooden blocks A-Z,
just as your loops with shoe
laces never quite fit my hand,
granny knot the usual failed
attempt – to this day give me
boot, slipper or buckle – what holds
without a line to grip me in knots.
At eight I would prove a man,
leaning to sight along the barrel
of the 12-gauge you held smiling,
the group of men squatted, waiting
the shot that sent me breathless,
reeling backward from the silent,
knowing faces, my shoulder stinging
into ache beyond the worst kick,
that purple patch of betrayal
hanging for weeks above my heart.
At thirteen my buddies the two beagles
you brought home as pups, penned
out back, hungry to break free,
lay back their ears in a lope,
trail every luring scent:
a mile from home, noses to ground,

you found them, jerked each up
by an ear, swung them like feed sacks,
yelps and howls worse than my screams,
rage doubled by your threat to swing
me by an ear if I didn't shut up.
Was it their yen for freedom
you hated, the leap to wild abandon
beyond your discipline forever?
So I believed returning home
from college when a friend told
me your belief that I was
ruined by books, words you claimed
were back talk and sass, so set free,
no longer to be the son
you wanted, words burning my ears
all these years. So forgive me, Father,
for even now I cannot forgive you.

CODAS

"What you see is what you get."
Such codas we learned from exotic
sources, say the carnival barker lining
his olive-skinned girls on stage outside the tent,
their little hoochie-koochie twists
and bumps luring us in to the hope
of some imagined Casbah. "Just a hint,
boys, of what you'll see inside." Room led to room
like every mystery, until our pockets emptied
of loose change, and we still had not seen it all.
So it was with my father's junkhouse,
so much to see and so little
time to take it all in: rows of jars
loaded with rubber washers, gaskets,
nuts and bolts, brass wood screws,
steel ball bearings so shiny I could feel
the silky roundness of them turning
between my fingers, a few slipped to school
for trade as we scrawled with shoetip
the ovals and rings in the dust of marble
season. How did he know what had been moved
and placed back so carefully, a PT boat
piston cut in half and fashioned
into an ashtray (his relic from the war
years of working for Alcoa in Detroit), only two
ball bearings taken from the jar and clacking
in my pocket? At ten I believed it was
the immaculate order in the mind of God,
His eye on each and every sparrow. "Son,
you don't need to be messing with the things

70

in my house." And so I learned not to tamper,
to look but not to touch. Until I turned fourteen
and he handed me his .22 automatic rifle:
at the dump site I watched him
drop rats on the run, never more than
a single shot. He lined five beer bottles
against the red clay bank. "First you shoot
the lip off, then the neck, and last you take
the easy gut shot." Long ago I had heard
the legend around town: "Boy, your old man
could shoot the hairs off a chigger's ass."
Our first trip into the field,
"See that rabbit hiding over behind the cedar –
take him when I flush him out." I stared
and stared and finally saw the tip of one ear
peeking through the cedar. Gut shot, he flopped
down the bank. My father turned his back
to me, lifted the rabbit by its hind legs,
and stilled its spasms with one quick blow
to the head. He thought I did not see
and through all the years we never spoke
of it. But today, standing in his junkhouse
ten years past his dying, I lift from memory
that old tattered scrap "what you see
is what you get," look at all these treasures
he laid up, and bow to every moment of his mercy.

RETURNABLE BOTTLES

They're a vanishing species, everything disposable now,
the neat convenience of toss-away cans –
but I remember bottlecaps you brought home
to me, my treasure of colorful coins, checkers
for countless games, prize messages hidden beneath
the cork lining. And cast on the bottles' glass
bottoms their place of origin, an exotic geography –
Marion, Alabama, the ones I searched for,
the plant and town I imagined named
for and owned by a distant cousin who someday
would share his many riches. Coke and Cherokee
Grape, Strawberry and Lemonade only a sampling
of what you stocked in the machines, an extra
duty assumed at the printing plant where you mixed
inks and matched colors for those thousands of labels,
every grocery shelf lined with your handiwork.
It was those drinks that put you through college
I learned, recalling the rounds we made on weekends
to gather empties scattered willy-nilly about the plant:
Why them boys can't put bottles back in the racks
beats me, you frowned, face red as a Campbell's
soup label when cigarette butts floated in a pool
of last dregs. Weekdays you made the rounds alone,
up three floors and back down, refilling machines,
gathering the empties on your breaks while I sat
far away allowing words to sweep me into worlds
beyond Marion, Alabama, into kingdoms of imagination
made possible by a man gathering bottles, his daily

journeys the worn paths of love trod over
and over, believing in my future he could not see,
but never receiving my message sent too late,
cast in this returnable Marion bottle.

Jeff Daniel Marion, a native of Rogersville, TN, has published seven poetry collections, four poetry chapbooks, and a children's book, *Hello, Crow*. His poems have appeared in *The Southern Review, Southern Poetry Review, Shenandoah, Atlanta Review, Epoch, Tar River Poetry*, and many others. From 1975-80, he edited *The Small Farm*, a distinguished regional poetry journal he founded. In 1978, Marion received the first Literary Fellowship awarded by the Tennessee Arts Commission. His previous book, *Ebbing & Flowing Springs: New and Selected Poems and Prose, 1976-2001* (Celtic Cat Publishing, 2002), was winner of the 2004 Independent Publisher Award in Poetry and was named Appalachian Book of the Year by the Appalachian Writers Association. Marion and his wife, poet and editor Linda Parsons Marion, live in Knoxville.

Printed in the United States
213161BV00002B/23/P